Britain's Greatest for Gallantry in t First World War

The story of the seven highest awards for valour in the First World War from the Victoria Cross to the Distinguished Conduct Medal.

by Stewart Binns

with a foreword by Sir Geoffrey Pattie

ISBN: 978-1-64440-325-9

Published by Inspire Creative, PO Box 59, Axminster EX13 9AH.

Edition reference 180829v6

Contents

Foreword

As a former serviceman and Honorary Colonel of the 4th Royal Green Jackets, I'm constantly reminded of the courage of those who serve our country both today and in past conflicts.

This year we mark one hundred years of the Armistice at 11am on 11/11/1918 that brought an end to the First World War.

With all those who fought in that great conflict no longer with us, it would be all too easy to simply forget the courage of those who sacrificed so much for 'King and Country' so many years ago. However, this year's commemoration needs to impress upon a whole new generation its ongoing significance.

This book tells the story of Britain's seven highest awards for gallantry during the First World War. These medals are an enduring reminder of exceptional acts of courage and self-sacrifice on the part of those to whom they were awarded. However, they should also be a reminder of the courage of all who served their country and faced the enemy in that conflict. Bravery has many forms, and I suspect that many acts of incredible courage went un-recorded and are therefore today, unrecognised.

The medals awarded do serve as a focal point, reminding us of a considerable number of gallant acts. Recounting the tales behind their award is one way we can preserve the memory of all those who have given so much.

signature

ssafa
—— the ——
Armed Forces
charity

Sir Geoffrey Pattie, former Minister of State
for Defence Procurement and Honorary Colonel
of the 4th Royal Green Jackets.

Opposite: King George V congratulates Lt. Cecil Leonard Knox after presenting him with the Victoria Cross. On 22 March 1918 at Tugny-et-Pont, Aisne, France, Second Lieutenant Knox was entrusted with the demolition of 12 bridges. He successfully carried out this task, but in the case of one steel girder bridge the time fuse failed to act, and without hesitation he ran to the bridge under heavy fire, and when the enemy were actually on it, he tore away the time fuse and lit the instantaneous fuse, to do which he had to get under the bridge. As a practical civil engineer, Second Lieutenant Knox would have understood the grave risk to his own life in taking this action.

Introduction

There have been rewards for valour for as long as we have had armies and wars in which they fought. Battles are won by brave soldiers, so it is not surprising that courage is rewarded by prestigious badges of honour.

As early as the Egyptian Old Kingdom (from the 3rd Dynasty through to the 6th Dynasty, 2686–2181 BC), heroic deeds on the battlefield were recognised in the Order of the Golden Collar. The order was symbolised by the wearing of a golden bracelet or necklace. It was also recognised in ceremonial artefacts like daggers, axes, armlets and headdresses.

By the time of the New Kingdom (from the 16th century BC to the 11th century BC, covering the 18th, 19th and 20th dynasties), heroism was rewarded by the Golden Fly of Valour, or the Order

Opposite: Queen Ahhotep I recovering the body of her husband, Seqenenre Tao, after the battle with the Hyksos after which she was granted the Ancient Egyptian 'Order of the Golden Fly' for her bravery.

9

of the Golden Fly. It is recorded that Queen Ahhotep, who lived c.1560–1530 BC, at the end of the 17th Dynasty, was granted the Order of the Golden Fly for her bravery in defending Thebes from the Hyksos people who had occupied northern Egypt. Ahhotep ruled Egypt as regent while she raised her son, Ahmose, the pharaoh who founded the 18th dynasty. Ahmose's funerary stele, recovered from Karnack, encouraged his people to revere his mother as, "one who has accomplished the rites and taken care of Egypt: She has looked after her soldiers, she has guarded her people, she has brought back her fugitives and gathered together her deserters, and she has pacified Upper Egypt and expelled her rebels."

It is interesting to reflect that the honours given to the first named warrior in history to be recognised for gallantry were bestowed on a woman: three golden fly pendants, a battle axe, and two models of ceremonial Bark. They were found in her tomb, part of the funerary and ritual objects symbolising: "the eternal victory of order over the enemies or evil forces."

It is known that the British Celts honoured their warriors, as did the Greeks of antiquity. Roman soldiers of distinction were honoured through a codified system of awards in the form of bronze or silver insignia that could be worn on the armour of the recipient. Roman military prowess is well known and it is typical of them that they developed a regularised honours system. Perhaps the best example was the Hasta Pura, although little detail has survived about its nature and to whom it was awarded. The hasta was a spear-like weapon, but not a throwing weapon like the later pilum, which was used like a javelin. 'Pura' denotes that it was a 'spear without iron', but why this symbolised bravery is not clear.

Tacitus, the 1st Century Roman historian, tells us that a Hasta Pura was bequeathed to a soldier for saving the life of a fellow-citizen: "In this engagement, Rufus Helvius, a common soldier, won the honour for saving a citizen's life, and was rewarded by the senator Apronius with a torc and a spear. To these the Emperor Tiberius added the Civic Crown."

The Civic Crown was a decoration awarded during the Roman Republic and the subsequent Principate, regarded as the second highest accolade to which a citizen could aspire. It took the form of a garland of oak leaves woven to form a crown.

The highest Roman decoration was, strange as it may seem, the somewhat uninspiringly named, Grass Crown. It was presented only to a general or officer whose actions saved a legion or the entire army. It was a garland made from what could be found on the battlefield, including grasses, flowers and crops and presented to the recipient by the army he had saved. Two of the most famous recipients were the generals, Scipio Africanus, who defeated Carthage in 146 BC, and Lucius Sulla, who marched on Rome in 82 BC to restore the power of the Senate.

Awards for bravery in battle began to appear again in the Middle Ages. The oldest still in use are Sweden's För tapperhet i fält ('For Valour in the Field') and För tapperhet till sjöss ('For Valour at Sea') awarded to officers and soldiers of the Swedish Armed Forces. The medals were introduced by King Gustav III in 1789, during his war against Russia. Although technically still active, Sweden's neutrality has led to it not being awarded since 1915.

The Austro-Hungarian Tapferkeits Medaille (Honour Medal for Bravery) has a similar story. Also introduced in 1789, by the Emperor, Joseph II, it was last awarded in 1945 to German ground-attack pilot, Hans Ulrich Rudel, the most decorated German servicemen of the Second World War, the only man to win the Knight's Cross of the Iron Cross with Golden Oak Leaves, Swords, and Diamonds.

Another of the world's oldest military decorations still in use is

The Fight for the Royal Standard at the Battle of Edge Hill English Civil War 23 October 1642. In the battle, the Royal Standard-Bearer, Sir Edmund Verney, was killed and the standard taken. Sir Robert Welch and Sir John Smith recovered it and were knighted on the field the next day by King Charles I, and later awarded a gold medal.

Poland's Order Wojenny Virtuti Militari ('The War Order for Military Valour'). It was first awarded in 1792 by King Stanislav II and last conferred in 1989. Perhaps its most famous recipient was Georgy Zhukov, Marshal of the Soviet Union, who was honoured in 1945 after the defeat of Nazi Germany.

The first British accolades for distinguished conduct in battle were, in effect, 'unofficial' accolades and can be traced back to the Civil War of 1642-1651. Known as 'reward badges' and mainly cast in silver, some of which have survived, they included the Earl of Manchester's Medal and Sir Thomas Fairfax's Medal. Sir Robert Welch and Sir John Smith were each given a gold medal after the Battle of Edgehill in 1642. In the Battle, the Royal Standard-Bearer, Sir Edmund Verney, was killed and the Standard taken. Smith and Welch recovered it and they were knighted on the field the next day by King Charles I.

In the middle of the 17th century, there was a brief period when a more systematic approach to British gallantry awards emerged with the Commonwealth Naval Medals of 1649-50 and 1658, specifically designed to acknowledge bravery at sea. This development faltered in 1660 with the restoration of Charles II, but in 1665, during the Dutch Wars, Naval Rewards appeared again under his reign and were continued under William and Mary.

However, there was no sustained expansion and, once again, honours became ad hoc and disorganised. Regiments, regimental officers, wealthy individuals, public subscriptions and well-meaning societies issued medals throughout the 18th century, especially during major conflicts like the French Wars of 1793-1815.

Nevertheless, we can be sure that the recipients were no less worthy than those recognised under more formal arrangements.

The Honourable East India Company should take the credit as the instigator of a standardised system of British decorations. In 1857, it inaugurated the Indian Order of Merit for its Indian soldiers. There were three classes and at least one notable recipient: Subedar Kishanbir Nagarkoti, IOM, 5th Gurkha Regiment (Rifles), the only person to have been awarded the IOM four times. He received the 3rd Class IOM for gallantry in the fighting in the Mangiar Pass in Afghanistan in 1878, was advanced to the 2nd Class for his actions at the Battle of Charasia in 1879 and then to the 1st Class for his bravery at Kabul, again in 1879. Then Nagarkoti posed the authorities a considerable problem when as a Subedar, he was again recommended for his outstanding gallantry in a rear-guard action during the Hazara campaign of 1888. But there was no class of IOM left to give him – so the authorities decided the unique expedient of awarding Nagarkoti a gold bar to his gold IOM.

It was the Crimean War of 1854 –1856, the first major conflict involving Britain for thirty-nine years, which finally roused the British out of their stupor and persuaded them to establish a structured series of gallantry awards. Up to that point, only officers were eligible for an award of one of the junior grades of the Order of the Bath, while a Mention in Despatches existed as an alternative award for acts of lesser gallantry.

These awards were grossly unfair. The Order of the Bath was confined to officers of field rank and Mentions in Despatches were largely confined to those who were under the immediate notice of the commanders in the field, generally members of the commander's own staff.

Other European countries had awards that did not discriminate against class or rank: France awarded the Légion d'honneur, established 1802, and The Netherlands gave the Order of William, established in 1815.

The severity of the Crimean conflict and the suffering endured by ordinary soldiers stirred the popular imagination, especially as the war was given widespread coverage by the first real war correspondents, notably William Howard Russell of The Times. Incidents like the now legendary Charge of the Light Brigade at Balaclava and the enduring and bloody Siege of Sebastopol led to demands for official recognition of the heroism shown by so many wearing the Queen's colours by awards that recognised incidents of gallantry regardless of the length or merit of a man's service.

Charles Davis Lucas was the very first recipient of the Victoria Cross: on 21 June 1854 during the Crimean War a live shell landed on the upper deck of his ship HMS Hecla. Lucas picked it up and threw it overboard just before it exploded, saving all on board.

Consequently, three new awards were instituted: The Distinguished Conduct Medal, for 'other ranks' of the army; The Conspicuous Gallantry Medal, open to 'other ranks' of the Royal Navy and Marines, as the naval equivalent of the DCM; and The Victoria Cross, for 'gallantry in the presence of the enemy'. The VC – For Valour, was open to all ranks of the Army, Royal Navy and Marines.

For the Crimean War, 111 VCs were awarded, at least 670 DCMs and 10 CGMs. 62 of the VCs were awarded by Queen Victoria in person. Britain's prestigious history of gallantry awards had begun.

Henry Tombs received the Victoria Cross for his actions when a major in the Bengal Horse Artillery, Indian Army during the Indian Mutiny. On 9 July 1857 at the Siege of Delhi, India, Major Tombs twice went to the rescue of one of his junior officers (James Hills). On the first occasion one of the enemy was about to kill the young officer with his own sword when Major Tombs rushed in and shot the man. A second attack on the subaltern resulted in his being cut down with a sword wound to the head, and he would undoubtedly have been killed if Major Tombs had not put his sword through the assailant.

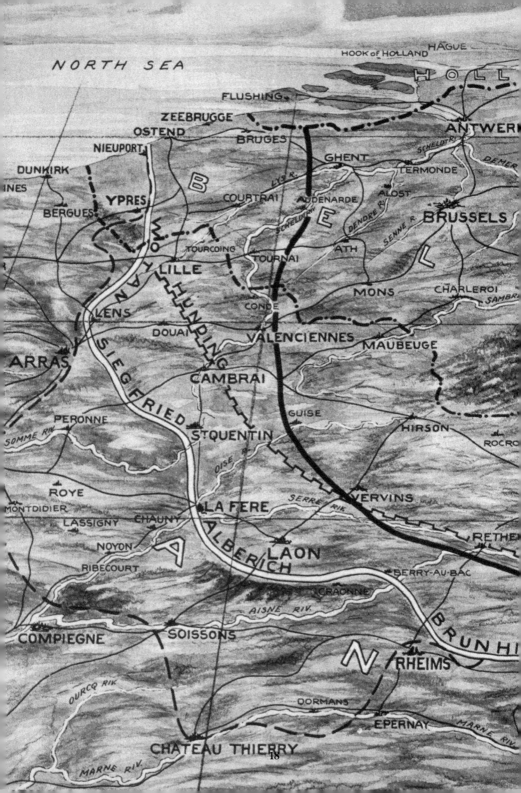

The Great War

As is well known, the enormity and tragedy of the Great War made it a uniquely extraordinary conflict. It was a slaughter on an unprecedented scale, a poignant loss of innocence and an all-too-graphic illustration, not only of brutal inhumanity, but also of courage and heroism.

These exceptional circumstances are reflected in the amazing number of awards for bravery that were granted and the remarkable individual stories behind them.

Many of the stories are well documented, but for some, all that is known is the brief citation in the London Gazette, in which all awards were notified.

The London Gazette is the official Journal of Record of the British Government. It has existed since 1665 and is still published today.

Opposite: World War One map of the Western Front showing the position of the opposing forces on Nov. 4, 1918, seven days before the armistice was signed. It also indicates the furthest point reached by the Germans, the Hindenburg Line.

Also, the gallantry awards were often recorded in the war diary of the man's unit. Most local newspapers carried stories of men receiving awards and after the war, books were published that gave extensive lists of men who had received honours.

While many gallantry and bravery awards were made to recognise a specific act and were granted immediately, large numbers were granted in the New Year's Honours and the King's Birthday Honours lists. These awards were often acknowledging

KING'S BIRTHDAY HONOURS LIST: TWO NE

IAT THE KING THINKS OF LORD KITCHENER.

TURKS AGAIN LOSE HEAVILY.

British In Close Hand-to-Hand Fighting In Dardanelles.

ENEMY'S ARTILLERY SUPPORT.

(FROM SIR IAN HAMILTON.)

nal Honour Bestowed Upon War Minister.

TWO BIRTHDAY PEERS.

ewards For Services During The War To Come Later.

Division of the First Class or Knight's Grand Cross—the Right Hon. Sir Rufus Daniel, Baron Raeding, K.C.V.O.

To be an additional member of the Civil Division of the Second Class or Knights Commanders—the Right Hon. Sir John Fletcher, Baron Moulton, F.R.S.

HEROES OF THE ARMY AND NAVY.

List Of 420 Awards Includes 100 Medals Won At Neuve Chapelle.

e King's answer to the unscrupulous cks on Lord Kitchener has been to bestow the great soldier one of the highest honours is power—the Knighthood of his Majesty, -day is the official birthday of his Majesty, the honour conferred upon the War Secre is the outstanding feature of the customary rds announced on the occasion.

Military honours fill 33 pages of last night's Gazette, and include the names of 420 officers and men. For gallantry and devotion to duty in the Dardanelles, 22 officers receive the Distinguished Service Order, while 14 officers and two non-commissioned officers are awarded the Military Cross. The Distinguished Conduct Medal is awarded to 55 non-commissioned officers and men for bravery in that theatre of the war, in East Africa, and Turkey-in-Asia, 327 Distinguished Conduct Medals are awarded.

The following official telegram regarding t operations in the Dardanelles was issued to t Press at Cairo yesterday:—

During the first of June close hand-to-har fighting occurred on our northern front.

At the northern section of our position in fro of what is known as Quinns Pov enemy were rushed by our men with the intent of filling them in, but heavy bombing checked t work, and one party had to fall back.

The other party still holds on to its positi between our firing line and that of the enemy. This action necessitated heavy artillery suppo to which the enemy replied vigorously regardi of expense.

Throughout this heavy fighting the enemy ag lost heavily.

On the southern section the Turks m repeated attacks during the night of the 1st 2nd against the French right, and twice reoccu the fort captured on May 29.

On both occasions the enemy were driven and the new French front remains intact.

On the British front all was quiet.

BALKAN ENTENTE COMING

Italy's Example Points The Danger Delay To Rival Powers.

PARIS, Wednesd

There are further hints in the Press this mo as to the possibility of a Balkan entente brought about.

KNIGHTHOOD FOR INDIAN POET.

It is announced in the Indian Honours list that the King has conferred a knighthood upon Mr. Rabindranath Tagore.

Mr. Tagore, the greatest of Indian poets, long ago won world-wide recognition, and two years back he was awarded the Nobel Prize for literature.

Since he was 19 years of age, when he produced his first novel, he has written many plays and poems, some of which have been translated into English. He is now 54 years of age.

New Barons.

The King's Birthday Honours List, 1915, included 420 medal awards, 100 of them won at Neuve Chapelle, a battle that had taken place on 10–13 March 1915. Of the 40,000 Allied troops in the battle, 7,000 British and 4,200 Indian casualties were suffered. 10 Victoria Crosses were awarded for excpetional valour.

a period of sustained gallant performance rather than a single act, and many went to those men who were not in a position to carry out spectacular deeds. For example, the men of the transport, artillery, medical and veterinary services, ordnance and engineering were often recognised retrospectively. The New Year's Honours were listed on December 31st or January 1st, and the King's Birthday Honours in June each year. Those gazetted in June 1919 are said to have been in the "Peace Gazette", as this issue approximately coincided with the conclusion of the Peace Conference at Versailles.

The following entry is typical of the tone of the citations and demonstrates how amazing acts of courage are reflected in just a brief mention on the pages of the London Gazette.

> Pte Alexander Adair, Royal Scots Fusiliers, gazetted January 12th 1920.

> "For conspicuous gallantry and devotion to duty on 1st October, 1918. The attack on the Faubourg de Paris being held up by heavy machine-gun fire, he with four men went forward to look for wounded. The four men became casualties, and he went on by himself, bandaging and carrying in wounded on his back. He kept on at his work all night, and showed an utter disregard for danger."

Adair received the Distinguished Conduct Medal.

22

The Distinguished Conduct Medal (DCM)

The Distinguished Conduct Medal was one of the three original gallantry medals declared in 1854 and is considered the oldest. Cast in silver, the reverse of the medal bears the inscription, For Distinguished Conduct in the Field, while the original Victorian obverse is the 'Trophy of Arms' design by Benedetto Pistrucci, the renowned Italian engraver and medallist. Pistrucci is best known for his 'St George and the Dragon' design for the British gold sovereign and his 'Waterloo Medal', a commission which took him 30 years to deliver, by which time most of its intended recipients had died.

A specimen medal was sent to Queen Victoria on January 29th 1855, who was delighted with it, and the War Office placed an order with the Royal Mint for a 1,000 to be struck. By the end of the year, 747 had been issued. In the United Services Gazette in March 1855, it reports, "We are glad to announce that these medals were

The Distinguished Conduct Medal of King George V (first type, issued until 1930)

forwarded to the Crimea this week. It is a very handsome medal." For many years, the DCM was highly-regarded and considered second only to the Victoria Cross as a reward for bravery.

The medal's ribbon is crimson with a wide blue stripe in the centre and is suspended from its ribbon by an ornate scrolled Bar. The obverse of the DCM was changed from the reign of Edward VII onwards to show the monarch's effigy and titles. All recipients are entitled to use the letters DCM after their name. Bars to the award were authorised in 1888.

Interestingly, not insignificant annuities were given with the medal. For example, in 1855 Staff-Sergeant George Marvin, Royal Horse Artillery, was awarded the DCM 'for services in the Crimea' and with it an annuity of £20; a handsome sum worth over £2,000 at today's values. Annuities for British gallantry awards are still paid to this day.

Of the 24,500 Great War DCMs, 472 included first Bars and nine second Bars. Approximately 1,900 DCMs were awarded during the Second World War, nine of which included first Bars.

In the aftermath of the 1993 review of the British honours system, which formed part of the drive to remove distinctions of rank in respect of awards for bravery, the Distinguished Conduct Medal was discontinued, as was the Conspicuous Gallantry Medal and the award, specifically for gallantry, of the Distinguished Service Order. These three decorations were replaced by the Conspicuous Gallantry Cross, to serve as the award for gallantry for all ranks of the Armed Service.

At the time of its discontinuation, over 29,800 medals had been awarded.

Sapper Frank Trask DCM
37th Field Company, Royal Engineers

One of the best-known recipients of the DCM was Sapper Frank Trask, who served during the Boer War with 37th Field Company, Royal Engineers.

He was awarded the medal for his bravery at Langerwachte Spruit on February 23rd 1900 for "coolness and gallant behaviour while making a sandbag wall under heavy fire." A report of the incident explained that Boers forces were in numbers higher up the Langerwachte valley, and that as soon as the head of the British column appeared on the bridge, they began a heavy rifle and pom-pom attack on it. The men crossed over in single rushes, but, even so, many were hit.

Trask, along with Company Sergeant Major John Smith, also from 17th Field Company, went out into the open to build the sandbag wall that gave vital cover from the enemy fire. Smith was also awarded a DCM.

Slightly less than 3,000 DCMs were awarded up to the outbreak of the Great War of 1914 – 1918, during which more than 24,500 were awarded. The high count led to some speculation that the number of awards was devaluing the prestige of the honour. Therefore, the Military Medal for bravery in battle on land was instituted in March 1916, as an alternative award to the Distinguished Conduct Medal. The lesser Military Medal was usually awarded for bravery from this date and the Distinguished Conduct Medal was reserved for exceptional acts of bravery.

Corporal John Windell DCM
2nd Battalion South Lancashire Regiment

One of the most famous acts of bravery which won the DCM was the actions of Corporal John Windell of the 2nd Battalion South Lancashire Regiment. On a misty morning at the end of October 1914, Windell was positioned to the east of Neuve Chapelle, engaged in mounting a machine-gun in the roof of a farm house. At that point, the news came that a strong force of Germans was approaching. An officer told Windell that a Maxim gun had been left in a house just in advance of the abandoned trenches. So, accompanied by the officer and a private, Windell left the farm and ran across the four hundred yards to open ground, which lay between them and the abandoned Maxim. They reached the house safely, to be greeted by, propped up against the wall, the lifeless body of the machine-gun sergeant of their battalion. Rushing up to the roof, where the Maxim was mounted, they saw that a considerable number of the enemy were advancing in massed formation.

A fierce encounter then ensued with Windell inflicting heavy casualties on the advancing Germans before engaging in a duel with a nearby German machine-gun position, which he put out of action, by which time he had emptied twelve boxes of ammunition. The German artillery then began to shell Windell's position and he and his colleagues had to abandon their position, leave the gun, and make their way across the open ground to safety. However, after half an hour Windell decided the enemy fire had subsided a little and, on his own initiative, went back to the house, and found the Maxim had sustained no damage. He then succeeded in getting it back to the British trenches.

Cpl George Thompson DCM
2nd Battalion, King's Own Scottish Borderers

Corporal George Thompson of the 2nd Battalion, King's Own Scottish Borderer enlisted in August 1914.

He was wounded during the Battle of Loos which took place from 25 September – 8 October 1915 on the Western Front. It was the biggest British attack of 1915, the first time that the British used poison gas and the first mass engagement of New Army units. The French and British tried to break through the German defences in Artois and Champagne and restore a war of movement. Despite improved methods, more ammunition and better equipment, the Franco-British attacks were contained by the German armies, except for local losses of ground. British casualties at Loos were about twice as high as German losses.

He received the Distinguished Conduct Medal and the citation in the London Gazette on 6 February 1918 reported:

The ruins of Loos, Belgium, after the Battle that bears its name

'for conspicious gallantry and devotion to duty in working round the flank and capturing an enemy strong point which was holding up the company. In it were about fifty of the enemy. He afterwards beat off with loss all counter-attacks on his trench'

Thompson was killed in action in April 1918.

Sergeant F. C. Clark DCM
1st Battalion, King's Shropshire Light Infantry

Another acclaimed Great War DCM was granted in March 1918. It was given to Sergeant F. C. Clark, 1st Battalion, King's Shropshire Light Infantry. Clark was holding a trench defending Battalion HQ at Lagnicourt, north-east of Bapaume. Although under intense shell and machine-gun fire, he managed to direct significant fire onto the enemy, inflicting many casualties. When running out of ammunition, rather than retreat, he went forward to retrieve more ammunition that had been abandoned and continued to fight. He only left the position when all but surrounded and fought a rearguard position to a safer trench. When all the officers nearby became casualties, Clark took charge and repeatedly went out into open ground to rescue wounded men.

The Air Force Cross (AFC)

Before 1918, personnel of the Royal Flying Corps, the air arm of the British Army and of the Royal Naval Air Service, the equivalent air arm of the Royal Navy, were awarded the appropriate gallantry awards from either the Army or the Navy.

Soon after the amalgamation of the two services with the

Captain Steven Jones with the Air Force Cross presented to him by The Queen on 16th Febraury 2012. An Apache helicopter pilot with the Army Air Corps, Jones heard a radio call for urgent assistance while returning to base after a full day of operations in Afghanistan in December 2010. An infantry patrol had been caught in an IED blast, which had killed one soldier and seriously wounded several others. The explosion's blast had also disabled the soldiers' radios - except the one that communicates with aircraft. Only helicopters in the air on the right frequency would be able to hear the soldiers' transmissions. Captain Jones, despite being dangerously low on fuel, kept the Apache in the air, and stayed in touch with the soldiers on the ground until an emergency response helicopter could reach the injured personnel and another helicopter could be raised to take over his watch. Captain Jones' citation reads: This single act enabled a swift response to a situation that would otherwise have been delayed, demonstrating his selfless dedication to the support of ground forces.

formation of the Royal Air Force in April 1918, awards were announced for gallantry in the service of the RAF.

The Air Force Cross was established on June 3rd 1918, the birthday of King George V, and is awarded to officers and warrant officers of the RAF for an act of valour and courage or devotion to duty performed whilst flying, though not in active operations against the enemy. It may also be granted to individuals not belonging to the RAF for having rendered distinguished services to aviation in actual flying. The Distinguished Flying Cross and the Distinguished Flying Medal were also introduced on the same day.

Since the 1993 review of gallantry awards, the AFC is now available for all ranks of the RAF services. A Bar is awarded for an additional act which would have warranted the AFC. The Bar has an eagle in the centre and the year of the award is engraved on the reverse. The AFC was originally awarded to Air Force commissioned officers and Warrant Officers, but this was expanded after the Second World War to include Army and Navy aviation officers, and again in 1993 to other ranks.

The Air Force Cross is struck in silver and consists of a thunderbolt in the form of a cross, the arms conjoined by the wings, the base Bar terminating with a bomb surmounted by another cross composed of aeroplane propeller blades, with the end of the four blades inscribed with the Royal Cypher G (top), R (left), VI (bottom) and I (right). The top arm is ensigned by a crown. In the centre of the obverse is a roundel displaying Hermes, mounted on a hawk in flight, bestowing a wreath. On the reverse of the award, within a central circle, the Royal Cypher GV, GVI, EIIR are engraved, above the date 1918, the year when the award was instituted.

The medal is suspended by a straight silver bar, ornamented with sprigs of laurel connected to the cross by a silver link. The design was created by Edward Carter Preston, a renowned Liverpool sculptor and medallist who designed a major series of sculptures and reliefs for the Liverpool Anglican Cathedral. The AFC is issued unnamed, but several of them were privately engraved by the recipient or their next of kin.

The ribbon consists of alternating red and white stripes leaning to the left at 45 degrees. Until 1919, the stripes were horizontal.

In total, 679 AFCs were awarded in 1918–1919 and a further 100 between 1920 and 1937. A further 2001 were won during the years of the Second World War, 1940–1945.

Among the many deserving stories that led to the award of an Air Force Cross are the accounts of Willie Read, George Bulman and Stanley Cockerel.

Lieutenant William (Willie) Read AFC
Royal Air Force

Lieutenant William (Willie) Read, Royal Air Force, was, gazetted on January 1st 1919. He was one of the very few to receive the AFC and 2 Bars. Read was commissioned a second lieutenant in the Hampshire Carabiniers, a yeomanry regiment, in September 1906. In March 1907, after leaving Cambridge, he transferred to the 1st (King's) Dragoon Guards.

After obtaining his pilot's licence in April 1913, Read was seconded to the Royal Flying Corps as a pilot in April 1914 and joined 3 Squadron. He was promoted lieutenant in June 1914.

Read accompanied his squadron to France in August 1914 and was wounded in December. In February 1915, he was appointed a flight commander in the Royal Flying Corps with the temporary rank of captain. In December 1915 he was sent home to organise 45 Squadron, returning to France in command in April 1916.

He was awarded the Military Cross in January 1916 and promoted to captain in August 1917. He became the first commanding officer of 104 Squadron, a bomber unit, in September 1917 with the acting rank of major. He was awarded the Air Force Cross (AFC) on January 1st 1919 and the Distinguished Flying Cross (DFC) on June 3rd 1919 for services in France.

After the war he served in Palestine with 216 Squadron from 1919 to 1921 and received a Bar to his AFC in July 1920. By October 1921, he had been promoted to squadron leader in the RAF, although still holding the rank of captain in the Army, and was in command of 216 Squadron. In November 1921, he finally transferred from the Army to a permanent commission in the Royal Air Force. He was awarded a second Bar to his AFC in the 1922 New Year Honours.

He was promoted wing commander in January 1924 and in March 1931, was appointed Inspector of Recruiting for the RAF. He retired in May 1932, on his 47th birthday and died in 1972.

Willie Read's 104 Squadron flew the Airco DH9, a light bomber two-seater biplane, during World War One. From 1920 this plane became known as the de Havilland DH9. Shown here are two DH9A aircraft, a modified version from 1918 which had a more powerful engine.

Paul Ward Spencer (George) Bulman AFC
46 Squadron and 3 Squadron Royal Flying Corps

Paul Ward Spencer (George) Bulman transferred from the Honourable Artillery Company to the Royal Flying Corps early in the Great War, serving in 46 Squadron and 3 Squadron. He was awarded the Military Cross in February 1918 for his services flying Sopwith Camels at the Battle of Courtrai with the following citation: "For conspicuous gallantry and devotion to duty. On five occasions; in most difficult weather conditions, he dropped bombs and fired on enemy infantry from a low altitude, inflicting heavy casualties. During these flights he frequently obtained valuable information, and twice drove off enemy machines which attempted to interfere. He showed the greatest initiative and resource." Later that year, he was awarded the Air Force Cross.

In July 1920 he was awarded a Bar to his AFC for services as a test pilot, and then in the 1922 Birthday Honours he was awarded a second Bar. In 1924, he won the Grove Prize for aeronautical research and in 1943 was appointed Commander of the Order of the British Empire (CBE). He married in 1920.

His only child, Flying Officer Raymond Paul Bulman, was killed in action over Germany in 1945, aged 21, while flying with 605 Squadron RAF. George Bulman died in 1963.

Captain Stanley Cockerell AFC
Royal Air Force

Captain Stanley Cockerell, Royal Air Force, was gazetted on July 20th 1920. He was a Royal Flying Corps aircraft mechanic before becoming a fighter pilot. He achieved seven aerial victories while flying the Airco DH.2, DH.5 and Sopwith Camel. After the war, he attempted the first flight from Cairo to Cape Town as a test pilot for Vickers, for which he was awarded the AFC. Cockerell and his daughter, aged only 6, were killed during the Luftwaffe bombing of Sunbury-on-Thames in November 1940.

Above and opposite: The Royal Air Force is the 'youngest' of the three armed forces, being founded in April 1918, from the amalgamation of the Royal Flying Corp and the Royal Navy Air Service. These two scenes showing the assmebly of aircraft from Fanborough in 1917, show the limited nature of aircraft production at that time. The Air Force Cross was instituted in June 1918 just a few months before the end of World War One.

The Distinguished Flying Cross (DFC)

The Distinguished Flying Cross is the combat equivalent to the Air Force Cross and intended for "An act or acts of valour, courage or devotion to duty performed whilst on active operations against the enemy."

The DFC was established on June 3rd 1918, by the same warrant that established the AFC. It was originally awarded to RAF commissioned and warrant officers. During the Second World War it was also awarded to Royal Artillery officers serving on attachment to the RAF as pilots-cum-artillery observers. Since the

Opposite: the prestigious DFC that was awarded to Group Captain Ivan Whittaker a member of the famous 617 "Dam Busters" squadron, who retired from the RAF as a group captain in 1974, but died five years later and remains the only flight engineer to be twice awarded the Distinguished Flying Cross. His first award, received in November 1943, was for taking part in daring and hazardous operations - including the attack on dams along the Ruhr. He received a second a year later after landing a plane with badly wounded legs following a raid over France.

Second World War, the award has been open to army and naval aviation officers, and to other ranks since 1993. Recipients of the Distinguished Flying Cross are entitled to use the letters 'DFC'.

The design of the DFC is a highly ornate medal in silver. Like its parallel award, the AFC, the DFC was created by Liverpool sculptor, Edward Carter Preston. The obverse of the Cross has flaming bombs at the end of three arms and a rose at the end of the upper one. Superimposed on this is a propeller, at the centre of which is a winged rose below a crown with 'RAF'. The reverse is, like the AFC, plain save for a roundel with the reigning monarch's monogram and the date of the institution of the honour, '1918'.

For the first few years of its life, the medal was struck by medal specialists, John Pinches Ltd of London, but thereafter by the Royal Mint. The ribbon for the medal is alternate horizontal stripes in violet and white, running diagonally at a 45° angle. The ribbon supports a silver suspension Bar decorated with sprigs of laurel, connected to the cross by a silver link.

The DFC is issued unnamed, but, like the AFC, they are often engraved by the recipient or their relatives.

During the Great War almost 1,100 DFCs were awarded, with 70 first Bars and 3 second Bars.

During the Second World War, 20,354 DFCs were awarded, the most of any award, with approximately 1,550 first Bars and 45 second Bars.

Perhaps the most renowned holder of a World War One DFC is Harold Whistler.

Harold Alfred Whistler DFC
3 Squadron and 80 Squadron Royal Flying Corps

The son of a Lincolnshire clergyman, Harold Alfred Whistler passed out from Sandhurst and was commissioned as a second lieutenant in the Dorsetshire Regiment in July 1916. He subsequently transferred to the Royal Flying Corps, to be trained as a pilot, and was seconded to the RFC in September as a flying officer. He was wounded in action on January 29th 1917, when he was with 3 Squadron RFC, but recovered to join 80 Squadron RFC. In January 1918, he returned to operations in France, where he was credited with 23 victories (1 balloon, 13 aircraft destroyed, 9 'out of control') between March 1918 and October 1918, all while flying Sopwith Camels.

At the end of the war, he stayed in the RAF as an instructor. In the late 1920s he commanded 55 Squadron in operations against the Najd Bedouin tribesmen in Iraq and was promoted to squadron leader in 1927. By 1940, he was Chief of Staff of RAF India as an acting Air Commodore. In March 1940, on a return trip to the United Kingdom from India, his plane disappeared without trace over the Gulf of Oman.

Whistler's gazetted citations make for impressive reading:

> August 3rd 1918. Lt. (temp. Capt.) Alfred Harold Whistler is awarded the Distinguished Flying Cross.

> "A very courageous and enterprising patrol leader, who has rendered valuable services. He has done exceptionally good work in attacking ground targets, which he engages at very low altitudes. During the past month his patrol attacked

eight enemy scouts who were flying above him. He attacked a triplane and brought it down in a crash, and whilst thus engaged another of his pilots destroyed a second enemy machine. The remainder of the enemy formation were then driven off."

November 2nd 1918

Capt. Alfred Harold Whistler, DFC (Dorset Regt.) is appointed a Companion of the Distinguished Service Order.

"During recent operations this officer has rendered exceptionally brilliant service in attacking enemy aircraft and troops on the ground. On 9 August he dropped four bombs on a hostile battery, engaged and threw into confusion a body of troops, and drove down a hostile balloon, returning to his aerodrome after a patrol of one and a half hours duration with a most valuable report. He has in all destroyed ten aircraft and driven down five others out of control."

February 8th 1919

Capt. Alfred Harold Whistler, DSO, is awarded a Bar to the Distinguished Flying Cross.

"This officer has twenty-two enemy machines and one balloon to his credit. He distinguished himself greatly on 29 September, when he destroyed two machines in one combat, and on 15 September, when, following two balloons to within twenty feet of the ground, he destroyed one and caused the observer of the second to jump out and crash. He has, in addition, done arduous and valuable service in bombing enemy objectives and obtaining information. Captain Whistler is a gallant officer of fine judgment and power of leadership."

March 15th 1929

Awarded a Second Bar to the Distinguished Flying Cross

"In recognition of gallant and distinguished services rendered in connection with the operations against the Akhwan in the Southern Desert, Iraq, during the period November 1927 – May 1928."

Warrant Officer G. S. H. Davies DFC
Royal Air Force Volunteer Reserve,
70, 104 and 622 Squadrons

George Samuel Henry Davies was born in Knowsley, Merseyside, in July 1914. He enlisted in the Royal Air Force Volunteer Reserve in August 1940 and carried out his initial training as an Air Gunner at RAF Harwell. He was posted overseas in October 1942, and joined 70 Squadron flying Wellington Bombers out of Abu Sueir in Egypt. Davies flew as a rear gunner in 13 operational sorties with the Squadron, mostly over 'Battle Area' targets during the North African Campaign, before being attached to 104 Squadron.

Davies served with 104 Squadron, again flying Wellingtons but this time out of Luqa in Malta, from December 1942. He flew in 8 operational sorties to targets in Tunisia, including one recorded in his log book: "31 December 1942. Ops Target Sfax (Harbour). Never to be forgotten. *One engine all the way home.*"

Davies returned to his parent Squadron, now based at Gardarbia West in Tunisia, in February 1943. He flew in a further 19 operational sorties with the Squadron, including a number against troops and armour concentrations during the Battle of the Mareth Line in March 1943, and similar targets during the Battle of Tunis in May 1943. Davies moved with the Squadron to Kairouan at the end of May, and took part in two attacks on Naples, including 16 June 1943.

Having completed his tour, Davies returned to the UK in August 1943. He served as an Instructor with No. 2 A.G.S., prior to returning to operational flying when he was posted to 622 Squadron, this time flying Lancaster Bombers, out of Mildenhall, in October 1944. Davies flew in 22 operational sorties with a number of crews, as either a rear gunner or a mid under gunner, to targets including Dortmund, Stuttgart, Clogne and Koblenz.

The recommendation to award him the DFC appeared in the London Gazette of 27 March 1945, and states:

'Warrant Officer Davies has now completed his 2nd tour of Operations throughout which he has performed his duties as an Air Gunner with exceptional skill and determination.

He arrived on the Squadron in September, 1944, having completed a successful 1st tour with 70 Squadron since when he has been employed as a spare gunner, flying with any crew as occasion demanded and the manner in which he has

A Wellington Mark IC of No. 38 Squadron, taxying before take-off at Luqa, Malta. Davies served with 104 Squadron, flying Wellingtons out of Luqa from december 1942 to February 1943. RAF operations from Luqa attacked German controlled targets in the Mediterranean and Italy.

accepted his responsibilities is worthy of the highest possible praise.

The keenness of W.O. Davies is best illustrated by the fact that in the short time since he joined the Squadron he has completed 22 sorties occupying 106.20 operational flying hours the majority of which have been against heavily defended German targets and notwithstanding the extreme hazard of these missions he has frequently volunteered his services in the best interests of the Squadron Operational effort.

By unselfish devotion to duty and total disregard to personal danger the example set by this Warrant Officer has been an inspiration to other gunners of the Squadron and is a fitting culmination to an outstanding operational career of 62 sorties. For sustained endeavour and gallantry in action I strongly recommend W.O. Davies for an award of the D.F.C.'

Davies was discharged in February 1946, and died in the village of his birth in 1974.

This shows how dangerous the position of Rear Gunner could be: the wrecked rear turret of a Lancaster Bomber of No. 57 Squadron after returning from a night raid to Oberhausen, Germany, in June 1943, during which it was attacked by German night fighters. The rear gunner was killed in this exchange.

Flight Lieutenant Michelle Jayne Goodman DFC
78 Squadron RAF

In 2008, Flight Lieutenant Michelle Jayne Goodman DFC became the first British woman to be awarded the Distinguished Flying Cross (DFC), for her actions while serving in Iraq, and the first female officer to be awarded any British combat gallantry medal.

Goodman joined the RAF in 2000, and, after initial officer training at Royal Air Force College Cranwell, she was appointed to a permanent commission as a pilot officer in 2000. In 2004 she trained as a helicopter pilot and joined 28 Squadron, part of the Merlin Force, transferring to 78 Squadron, when the Squadron was reformed in 2007. She completed three tours of Iraq.

Goodman was captain of an Incident Reaction Team Merlin, when, in June 2007, she flew into Basra at night using night vision and under heavy fire to evacuate a serious casualty, a 20-year-old Rifleman of the 4th Battalion The Rifles (who had been given 15 minutes to live following a mortar attack).

Her DFC was gazetted in March 2008. The citation for her DFC shows how things have changed since the citations for World War One, in terms of both the level of detail and also the appreciation of personal risk:

> The incident took place on 1 June 2007. At 2315 hours Flight Lieutenant Goodman was alerted that there was a serious casualty following a mortar attack on an isolated British location in the centre of Basra City. Landing an

A Royal Air Force Merlin on operations over Afghanistan. The Merlin (Bird of prey) HC3 and HC3a are operated by 78 Squadron. The Merlin is the first of a new generation of advanced, medium support helicopters for the RAF, and was the aircraft flown by Flt Lt Michelle Goodman DFC.

aircraft at this location is assessed to be very high risk and intelligence reports indicated a large, 'spectacular' attack would occur somewhere in Basra, with a helicopter being a possible target. Flight Lieutenant Goodman was fully aware of the elevated threat level.

Alert to the high risk, but being fully conscious of the importance of providing unfailing Instant Reaction Team (IRT) support to ground forces, Flight Lieutenant Goodman elected to fly her approach, whilst under intense enemy direct and indirect fire. Maintaining a firm control of the situation whilst flying tactically on Night Vision Goggles at very low level across a hostile city, she commenced a most expeditious transit and approach to an unfamiliar and dangerous landing site.

She continued her approach, undeterred by close friendly covering fire and even closer enemy fire which began to impact to the rear of the aircraft. Despite the most complex approach, with numerous obstructions and ambient conditions on the limit of aviation operations, she executed a landing with few visual references bringing the aircraft in next to the casualty. The medics and Aviation Reaction Force left the aircraft as four mortar rounds landed in and around the location; however, she remained in full control of the situation and elected to hold the aircraft on the ground as the option with least risk.

The top cover Lynx helicopter was by now reporting several substantial explosions in the area, which were believed to be either enemy mortars or Rocket propelled Grenade fire. With the casualties loaded, Flight Lieutenant Goodman departed the helicopter landing site just as further explosions occurred in close vicinity to the aircraft. Additionally, her aircraft detected possible enemy missile engagement and automatically discharged flares as a counter measure. She departed the area, her path covered by very close friendly artillery fire to distract enemy forces.

Flight Lieutenant Goodman flew rapidly from the area, making maximum use of the aircraft's performance, crew and supporting assets to achieve a safe transit clear of the area. The aircraft landed at the British Field Hospital just 14 minutes after launch. Many IRT sorties are high risk. However, on this occasion Flight Lieutenant Goodman had to instantly weigh up the risks against the importance of recovering a serious casualty, which would impact on morale throughout the coalition.

Without the IRT, the casualty would have died within 15 minutes. Despite extreme pressure, whilst in the face of the enemy, she made the right decision. This was a bold and daring sortie which undoubtedly saved life.

She retired from the Royal Air Force in 2012.

The Military Cross (MC)

The Military Cross was established by royal warrant on December 28th 1914 and the first awards were gazetted on January 1st 1915, for "gallant and distinguished service in action." 99 men received the award, the first of whom was Lieutenant G.F.H. Brooke, 16th Lancers. Brooke also won a DSO, eventually became a major general and was appointed Companion, Order of the Bath (CB). He died in 1982 at the age of 82.

The MC is a plain Greek cross, struck in silver, with splayed ends to each cross. The obverse of the ends of the crosses are decorated with the British imperial crown, with the reigning monarch's monogram in the middle.

The reverse of the MC is plain unless the recipient's details are privately engraved, except for the years between 1938 and 1957, when the year of the award was engraved on the lower arm. The

The Military Cross of Queen Elizabeth II (note the monarch's monogram at the centre of the medal)

ribbon is white with a central purple stripe, while the suspension bar is a plain, flat bar with a small ring attaching to the medal.

Originally, the MC was awarded to warrant officers and junior commissioned officers, but since 1993, it has been available to all ranks. Bars to the MC were granted after August 1916, which are a plain, flat slide-on Bar with a central crown.

A significant number of Military Crosses were issued during the Great War, a total approaching 40,000, of which, almost 3,000 men received a Bar, 168 a second Bar and four men a third Bar. Over 10,300 MCs were awarded during the Second World War.

Acting Captain Francis Victor Wallington of the Royal Field Artillery was the first person to be awarded the MC and three Bars when he was invested with his third Bar in July 1918. The three other officers subsequently awarded a third Bar were: Percy Bentley, Humphrey Arthur Gilkes and Charles Gordon Timms.

Percy Bentley MC
49th (West Riding) Infantry Division

Following the outbreak of the Great War, Percy Bentley was sent to France in April 1915, in the 148th (3rd West Riding) Brigade of the 49th (West Riding) Infantry Division. His battalion was moved to the 187th (2/3rd West Riding) Brigade of the 62nd (2nd West Riding) Division in February 1918.

He served as the battalion adjutant from 1915 to 1919, was promoted to the rank of temporary captain in June 1915 and then substantive captain in June 1916. He was wounded in 1915 and again at Passchendaele in 1917.

He was awarded his first MC in December 1916, a first Bar in September 1918, a second Bar in November 1918, and a third in January 1919 for his actions at the Battle of Havrincourt in September 1918. All four of his citations describe how he moved forward under heavy fire to organise and gather information. While the citation for his third Bar describes:

> For conspicuous gallantry and untiring energy as adjutant of the battalion at Havrincourt on 12th-14th September, 1918. After a most determined counter-attack, he went forward to the village to clear up an obscure situation, and, in spite of severe shelling, collected reports which, enabled the defences to be reorganised. Later, he made another reconnaissance of great value. Throughout the operations he was indefatigable, and showed great courage

Bentley resigned his commission in 1922, and became Mayor of Pontefract in 1930–31. He died at home in 1956.

Charles Gordon Timms OBE, MC
7th Battalion Royal Fusiliers

Charles Gordon Timms was born at Mount Hesse Station, near Winchelsea, Victoria, Australia, where his father owned a sheep farm. He went to Edinburgh University in 1907 where he played rugby for Edinburgh University and the British Lions touring team to South Africa in 1910.

In the war, Timms became a unit medical officer while attached to 7th Battalion Royal Fusiliers, having been awarded his captaincy on enlistment. The citation for Charles Timms' first Military Cross, gazetted on July 18th 1917 reads:

'For two days he attended the wounded in the open under heavy and incessant shell fire, quite regardless of personal danger, and his coolness and energy alleviated much suffering."

On July 26th 1918 his first Bar was gazetted.

"He continued to collect and evacuate wounded from his post, though several times nearly surrounded by the enemy and under heavy shell fire. By his fine courage and self-sacrifice, he was able to get away a large number of wounded under most difficult conditions."

A second Bar was gazetted on January 11th 1919:

"During a counter-attack this officer went forward from battalion headquarters and effected several rescues of seriously wounded men, conducting them personally to the lines. Throughout the week's fighting he worked night and day, and the manner in which he disposed stretcher cases under fire was admirable."

A third Bar was gazetted on February 1st 1919:

"Near Cambrai on 1st October 1918, during a severe enemy Barrage, when his CO was wounded, he at once took up a squad of stretcher-bearers into the Barrage to the rescue, tending his wounds and seeing that he was conveyed to a place of safety."

Timms joined the Colonial Medical Service after the war, serving in Uganda in 1922, and then in British Somaliland. He was appointed an Officer of the Order of the British Empire in the 1936 Birthday Honours for his service in Somaliland. He rejoined the Royal Army Medical Corps in 1939, with the rank of lieutenant. He died in 1956.

Humphrey Arthur Gilkes MC
47th London Division

Humphrey Arthur Gilkes joined the London Regiment and served with the 47th London Division. On September 17th 1917, the London Gazette announced the award of the MC:

> "As Battalion Intelligence and Signalling Officer, he made repeated reconnaissances under heavy fire, gaining valuable information and maintaining efficient communications throughout a period of several days."

On March 4th 1918, he was awarded a Bar to his MC:

> "He led a patrol to a strong point 500 yards in advance of our line to discover whether it was occupied by the enemy. Finding it unoccupied, he set fire to the dugout and blew up a store of bombs and ammunition. He showed great resource and initiative."

A second Bar was gazetted on June 22nd 1918:

> "Accompanied by an NCO, he entered the enemy's advanced line and captured four prisoners. On the following day he reconnoitred the ground in advance of the line for over 1,500 yards and discovered the enemy's dispositions. Later he reconnoitred over 2,000 yards of the front and obtained valuable information as to the enemy's movements. On the same day, when the situation was very obscure, he entered a village which was held by the enemy, reconnoitred it, and brought back valuable information. He showed magnificent daring and skill."

A third Bar was gazetted on February 1st 1919:

"For conspicuous gallantry at Moislains on September 2nd 1918. When an attack had partially failed, and the situation had become obscure, he made repeated reconnaissances through a very heavy Barrage, and over ground swept by machine-gun fire, regardless of his own safety, and it was owing to his accurate reports that timely action was taken to restore a critical situation. His courage and resource was most marked."

The History of the 47th London Division reports:

"Communications had become worse, as we were getting off the front network of telephone lines, and much had to be done by means of runner and despatch-rider. During the day much visual signalling had been done, the 140th Brigade keeping up communication all day with the Metz exchange by this means. The 15th Battalion, on the extreme right, had an anxious and heavy task to perform, and the fact that no Germans filtered through the gap throws great credit on the way in which the patrols and machine-gunners did their work that night. One of the officers attached to the 140th Brigade Headquarters (Lieutenant H. A. Gilkes, M.C.) went out alone to Dessart Wood and brought in two German prisoners, a piece of work typical of this gallant young officer, who won the rare distinction of three Bars to his Military Cross." March 22/23 1918.

Gilkes resigned his commission in 1923 and joined the Colonial Medical Service. After serving in Northern Rhodesia, he moved to Trinidad. With the outbreak of the Second World War and with the rank of Colonel, he joined the Royal Army Medical Corps and served in Somaliland as Principal Medical Officer. He was killed in an air crash on July 11th 1945 and was buried in Djibouti.

60

The Distinguished Service Cross (DSC)

The Distinguished Service Cross was originally instituted in 1901 as the Conspicuous Service Cross for junior commissioned officers and warrant officers of the Royal Navy for "meritorious or distinguished services in action." Only eight awards were made before 1910.

In October 1914, by Order in Council, it was re-named as the Distinguished Service Cross. In 1931, the award was extended to merchant and fishing fleets and in World War Two to Royal Air Force and British Army personnel serving afloat. As part of the 1993 reforms, the DSC became available to all ranks. It is now awarded for "Gallantry during active operations against the enemy at sea."

The DSC is a plain silver cross with convex ends to the arms. In a central roundel, only the cypher of the monarch is on the obverse. The reverse is plain, except that, after 1940, the year of the award is engraved on the lower arm. The medal is suspended by a plain silver ring from a ribbon of three equal stripes: dark blue, white and dark blue.

Bars were authorised in 1916 and are silver 'slip-on' types with convex ends to match the cross and are decorated with a central crown.

1,983 DSCs were awarded during the Great War, with 91 first Bars and 10 second Bars. 4,524 DSCs were awarded during the Second World War, with 434 first Bars and 44 second Bars. Since 1945, fewer than 100 DSCs have been awarded. There has only been one recipient of a third Bar. Three of the most prominent Great War DSC recipients were Thomas Le Mesurier, Richard Pearman Minifie and Norman Eyre Morley.

Thomas Le Mesurier DSC
211 Squadron RAF

Thomas Le Mesurier was commissioned as a sub-lieutenant in the Royal Naval Reserve in March 1915 and was confirmed in his rank of flight sub-lieutenant in the Royal Naval Air Service in July 1915.

Le Mesurier's first aerial victory came in June 1917 when he drove down out of control an Albatros D.III west of Bruges. His next came a few days later when he destroyed and drove down two more D.IIIs, after which he was promoted to flight commander.

When, in April 1918, the Royal Naval Air Service (RNAS) and the Army's Royal Flying Corps (RFC) were merged to form the Royal Air Force, Le Mesurier's rank of flight commander was converted to the RAF equivalent of captain. He was also transferred to 211 Squadron RAF (formerly 11 (Naval) Squadron).

His Distinguished Service Cross citations read as follows:

"For conspicuous work as a pilot of a bombing machine. Has taken part in fourteen raids and numerous fighter patrols."

Bar to the Distinguished Service Cross

"For consistent skill and courage in leading his flight on bombing raids, particularly on the 28th July, 1917."

Second Bar to the Distinguished Service Cross

"For gallantry and consistent good work. He has at all times displayed the utmost gallantry in action, and by his determination and skill has set a very fine example to the pilots of his squadron. On the 23rd April, 1918, in spite of bad weather conditions, he successfully dropped bombs on the

Ostend Docks from a height of 800 feet amidst very intense anti-aircraft and machine-gun fire. He also made valuable observations. He has taken part in many bomb raids, and has destroyed or driven down out of control several enemy machines."

On the morning of May 26th 1918, Le Mesurier was flying an Airco DH.9 on a test flight when he was attacked by German Marine guns and suffered severe damage to the aircraft. Le Mesurier managed to pilot the stricken aircraft back towards his own lines, but crashed after the port wing folded up crossing over the trenches at 20 feet. The aircraft was destroyed. Le Mesurier later died of the wounds he sustained and was buried in the Town Cemetery in Dunkirk.

Richard Pearman Minifie DSC
1 Wing RNAS

Richard Pearman Minifie was born in Alphington, Victoria, Australia in 1898. He won a scholarship to Trinity College at the University of Melbourne, but, in 1916, decided to postpone his studies and travel to the United Kingdom where he enlisted in the Royal Naval Air Service.

Granted the substantive rank of flight sub-lieutenant in October, he was posted to 1 Wing RNAS on graduating in October 1916. In early 1917, he was flying Sopwith Triplanes, an aircraft in which he was to score heavily.

Throughout February and March 1917, he was "continually in action" along the Somme sector of the Western Front. In an air battle in April, Minifie was credited with his first two aerial victories, shooting down an Albatros D.III in a solo effort, before sharing in the destruction of a second with a fellow Australian pilot. At 19 years of age, Minifie was the youngest Australian 'Ace' of the First World War (a military aviator credited with shooting down five or more enemy aircraft during aerial combat).

Cited for his efforts in bringing down several German aircraft and his assaults on ground targets between April and September, Minifie was awarded the Distinguished Service Cross in November 1917. Minifie was credited with a further eleven German aircraft, bringing his total to seventeen and at the end of November, he was awarded a Bar to his DSC as a consequence of his "conspicuous gallantry in air fighting that resulted in his personal destruction of several enemy machines."

In March 1918, he led a party of four aircraft out on a patrol. While airborne, the group intercepted a formation of five German scout planes. In the ensuing battle, Minifie destroyed two of the aircraft, raising his ultimate tally to twenty-one

Sopwith Triplanes from No. 1 (Naval) Squadron, Royal Naval Air Service, in Bailleul, France. The aircraft nearest the camera (N5454) was primarily flown by ace Richard Minifie

aircraft. As a result of his gallantry while operating against hostile forces, particularly in the air battle in March, Minifie was awarded a second Bar to his DSC. The citation reads:

> "For courage and daring in the face of the enemy, particularly on the 13th March, 1918. On that date, when on patrol with four machines, he attacked an enemy patrol of five scouts, destroying two. Act. Flt. Cdr. Minifie has now destroyed numerous hostile machines."

Later in March, Minifie was forced to crash land in German-held territory in Belgium and taken as a prisoner of war. He spent the remainder of the war at prison camps in Germany.

After the war, Minifie returned to civilian life in Australia, but in June 1941, Minifie enlisted in the Royal Australian Air Force for service in the Second World War, and was later appointed as commander of 1 Squadron, 1 Cadet Wing, reaching the rank of squadron leader. He died in 1969.

The Distinguished Service Order (DSO)

The Distinguished Service Order was instituted on September 6th 1886 by a Royal Warrant of Queen Victoria. The first DSOs awarded were dated November 25th 1886. The DSO is typically awarded to officers ranked major or higher, but the honour has sometimes been awarded to especially gallant junior officers.

The Order was established to reward individual instances of meritorious or distinguished service in war. It was a military order, until recently for officers only, and normally given for service under fire or under conditions equivalent to service in actual combat with the enemy.

However, between 1914 and 1916 it was awarded under circumstances which could not be regarded as under fire. For example, to staff officers, awards which caused resentment among front-line officers. In 1917, commanders in the field were

The Distinguished Service Order of King George V (note the monarch's monogram at the centre of the medal)

instructed to recommend this award only for those serving under fire.

A number of more junior officers were awarded the DSO, and this was often regarded as an acknowledgement that the officer had only narrowly failed to achieve the award of the Victoria Cross. In 1942, the award of the DSO was extended to officers of the Merchant Navy who had performed acts of gallantry while under enemy attack.

In the 1993 gallantry awards reforms, the DSO ceased to be an award for gallantry with the introduction of the Conspicuous Gallantry Cross. However, it was retained as an award for 'outstanding leadership' and open to any rank, but, despite the very demanding recent campaigns in Iraq and Afghanistan, it has yet to be awarded to someone of non-commissioned rank.

Recipients of the order are officially known as Companions of the Distinguished Service Order and are entitled to use the letters 'DSO' after their name.

The DSO medal is a gold silver-gilt cross, enamelled white and edged in gold. In the centre, within a wreath of laurel and enamelled green, is the imperial crown in gold upon a red enamelled background. The reverse bears the royal cypher in gold upon a red enamelled ground, within a wreath of laurel, enamelled green.

The suspension bar is in gold, decorated with laurel, while at the top of the ribbon - a red central stripe flanked by two narrow stripes of dark blue – there is a second gold Bar, also decorated with laurel.

The Bar for an additional award is plain gold with an Imperial Crown in the centre. The back of the Bar is engraved with the year of the award..

During the Great War, 8,981 DSOs were awarded. 708 were given a first Bar, 71 a second Bar and there were seven third Bars.

In the Second World War 4,880 DSOs were awarded.

The seven recipients of a third Bar to their DSO were: Archie Buckle, William Croft, William Dawson, Bernard Freyberg, Arnold Jackson, Robert Knox and Edward Wood.

Archibald Walter Buckle DSO
63rd (Royal Naval) Division

Archibald Walter Buckle was born in Chelsea, and became a school teacher at St Augustine's School in Paddington. He joined the London Division of the Royal Naval Reserve in 1908 and became a Petty Officer in 1912. He married Elsie Louise Meeks in 1914, but, when the Great War broke out, returned to London from his honeymoon to join his unit.

There was a surplus of naval personnel at sea at the beginning of the war, and Buckle served on land with the Royal Naval Division. He was involved in the defence of Antwerp in 1914 with the Drake Battalion. He went to the Western Front with the 63rd (Royal Naval) Division, which supported the 1916 Somme Offensive, fought at the Battle of Arras in April 1917 and then in the Third Battle of Ypres (Passchendaele) in October 1917. He went on to command the Anson Battalion in the Hundred Days Offensive in 1918.

Buckle's DSO was gazetted in March 1918 for actions during the Battle of Cambrai:

> "For conspicuous gallantry and devotion to duty. When in command of a battalion detailed to counter-attack, he carried out a daring reconnaissance, under extremely heavy artillery

fire, enabling him to form sound dispositions, which resulted in the recapture of an important position. Throughout the day his coolness and example inspired all ranks."

Buckle's first Bar was granted in July 1918:

"For conspicuous gallantry and devotion to duty when in command of a battalion. He repelled the enemy's attack, organised a counter-attack, and drove the enemy completely out of the menaced area. It was largely due to his courage, initiative and leadership that this important success was obtained."

In January 1919, Buckle's second Bar was gazetted:

"For conspicuous gallantry and devotion to duty. When the progress of the brigade at a critical moment was checked by machine gun fire, he went forward himself with his battalion staff, reorganised his battalion and led it forward on to commanding ground, seriously threatening the enemy's retreat. The success of the operation was largely due to his courage and fine leadership."

His third Bar appeared in March 1919:

"During the fighting round Niergnies on 8th October, 1918, he showed great courage and powers of leadership. After the enemy had counter-attacked and succeeded in entering our lines, he seized an enemy anti-tank rifle and engaged three hostile tanks with it and drove them off. He then rallied men of various units in his neighbourhood and led them forward to the positions whence they had been forced. Throughout he did excellent work."

William Denman Croft DSO
27th Infantry Brigade in the 9th (Scottish) Division

William Denman Croft was the third son of Conservative MP Sir Herbert George Denman Croft, 9th Baronet. He received a commission in the regular army with the Cameronians (Scottish Rifles) as a second lieutenant in March 1900. Seconded to the Colonial Office in 1903, he served in Nigeria, where, in 1907, he is said to have been wounded by a poisoned arrow.

At the beginning of the war, Captain Croft was serving as adjutant of the 5th Battalion of the Cameronians. By December 1915, he was temporary lieutenant colonel in command of the 11th Battalion of the Royal Scots, before, in September 1917, being promoted to temporary brigadier general to command the 27th Infantry Brigade, in the 9th (Scottish) Division. He remained in command until 1919. Croft was Mentioned in Despatches ten times.

In little over two years, from January 1917 to February 1919, he was awarded the DSO four times. He received his first DSO in January 1917 and a first Bar just nine days later. He received a second Bar in July 1918 and a third in February 1919.

He became a brevet lieutenant colonel in January 1918, a Companion of the Order of St Michael and St George (CMG) in January 1919, and an Officier of the Légion d'honneur in August 1919.

After the war, Croft published an account of his war service, under the title Three Years with the 9th (Scottish) Division, before retiring in 1934 with the rank of honorary brigadier general. He became a Companion of the Order of the Bath (CB) in 1935.

In the Second World War, Croft was a Home Guard commander in Cornwall, where he died in 1968 aged 89.

William Robert Aufrère Dawson DSO
6th 'Dawson's' Battalion Royal West Kent Regiment

William Robert Aufrère 'Bob' Dawson was born in Berkshire into a military family and studied law at Oriel College, Oxford, where he was a Cadet in the Officer Training Corps. He served with the Royal West Kent Regiment on the Western Front from June 1915, in the 12th Division, and commanded the 6th Battalion from 1916 until his death in 1918.

He refused staff appointments and the possibility of promotion to command a brigade so that he could remain with his battalion, which became known as 'Dawson's Battalion'.

Dawson was often wounded through leading from the front. He was wounded twice in 1916 and at Monchy near Arras in May 1917 but returned to command in August 1917. He was wounded again at Cambrai in November, resuming command in February 1918, before being wounded yet again in March in the German Spring Offensive. He returned to command in June 1918 for the Hundred Days Offensive but was severely wounded by a shell near Nivelle on October 23rd 1918. After a long period in the 20th General Hospital at Camiers, during which time he was visited by his parents, he died of wounds in December 1918. He was buried at Étaples Military Cemetery.

Mentioned in Despatches five times, his first DSO was gazetted in April 1916, with the first Bar in July 1917, a second Bar in June 1918, and a third Bar (posthumously) in March 1919.

Bernard Cyril Freyberg 1st Baron Freyberg,
VC, GCMG, KCB, KBE, DSO
Queen's (Royal West Surrey) Regiment

Bernard Cyril Freyberg was born in Richmond, Surrey of partial Austrian- German descent and moved to New Zealand with his parents at the age of two. A strong swimmer, he won the New Zealand 100-yards championship in 1906 and 1910.

In May 1911, Freyberg gained formal registration as a dentist and worked as an assistant dentist in Morrinsville and later practised in Hamilton and in Levin. Freyberg left New Zealand in March 1914.

A 1942 Life magazine article claimed that Freyberg went to San Francisco and Mexico around this time and was a captain under Pancho Villa during the Mexican Revolution. Upon hearing of the outbreak of war in Europe in August 1914, he travelled to Britain via Los Angeles (where he won a swimming competition) and New York (where he won a prize-fight), using his winnings to cross the United States and the Atlantic.

In England, he volunteered for service and joined the 7th Hood

Battalion of the Royal Naval Brigade and served on the Belgian Front in September 1914. In late 1914, he met Winston Churchill, then First Lord of the Admiralty, and persuaded him to grant him a Royal Naval Volunteer Reserve commission.

In April 1915, Freyberg became involved in the Dardanelles campaign. On the night of April 24th, during the initial landings by Allied troops, following the unsuccessful naval attempt to force the straits by sea, Freyberg volunteered to swim ashore in the Gulf of Saros. Once ashore, he began lighting flares so as to distract the defending Turkish forces from the real landings taking place at Gallipoli. Despite coming under heavy Turkish fire, he returned safely from this outing and for his action he received the DSO. He received serious wounds on several occasions and left the peninsula when his division evacuated in January 1916.

In May 1916 Freyberg was transferred to the Army as a captain in the Queen's (Royal West Surrey) Regiment. During the final stages of the Battle of the Somme, he commanded a battalion as a temporary lieutenant colonel at Beaucourt-sur-Ancre. After

Freyberg, as one of the commanders of allied forces in the Mediterranean, even had the ear of the Prime Minster, Winston Churchill, whom he had first met late in 1914 during World War One. They are shown here in 1942.

his battalion had carried the initial attack through the enemy's front system of trenches, he rallied his own men and some others, and led them on a successful assault of the second objective, during which he suffered two wounds. He remained in command and held his ground throughout the day and the following night.

When reinforced the next morning, he attacked and captured a strongly fortified village, taking 500 prisoners. Although wounded twice more, the second time severely, Freyberg refused to leave the line until he had issued final instructions. For his actions, he was awarded the Victoria Cross.

The citation for the award concludes with:

> "The personality, valour and utter contempt of danger on the part of this single Officer enabled the lodgement in the most advanced objective of the Corps to be permanently held, and on this point d'appui (support) the line was eventually formed."

During his time on the Western Front Freyberg continued to lead by example. His bold leadership had a cost: Freyberg received nine wounds during his service in France, and men who served with him later in his career said hardly a part of his body did not have scars.

He won a Bar to his DSO in September that year, before ending the war by leading a cavalry squadron detached from 7th Dragoon Guards to seize a bridge at Lessines, which was achieved one minute before the armistice came into effect, earning him a second Bar to the DSO. By the end of the war, Freyberg had added the Croix de Guerre to his name, as well

The Campaign in Italy during the Second World War. General Sir Bernard Montgomery (centre) with his senior officers at Eighth Army Headquarters; General Bernard Freyberg is immediately to the right of Montgomery.

receiving five mentions in despatches. With his VC and three DSOs, he is ranked among the most highly decorated soldiers of the First World War.

Freyberg went on to have an even more illustrious career in World War Two, when he won a third Bar to his DSO. As Major General, he commanded the New Zealand Expeditionary Force (1939–45) and commanded the Allied forces during the battle for control of Crete in 1941. In fighting near Minqār Qaⅻim in Egypt, in June 1942, Freyberg was wounded, but he recovered in time to lead the breakout at the Second Battle of El Alamein. An extremely competent commander, Freyberg later fought in North Africa and in Italy under generals Montgomery, Alexander, and the American Mark Clark.

In 1942 he received a knighthood and in 1946 became Governor-General of New Zealand, an appointment he held for six years. In 1951 he was created a Baron. He died at Windsor Castle, where he was Deputy Constable and Lieutenant Governor in Charge, in 1963, when one of his many wounds ruptured. He was aged 74.

Arnold Nugent Strode-Jackson CBE DSO
13th Battalion, The King's Royal Rifle Corps

Arnold Nugent Strode-Jackson was born at Addlestone Surrey. He was the grandson of Lieutenant General George Jackson. His uncle was Clement Jackson, athlete, academic, bursar of Hertford College, Oxford, and co-founder of the Amateur Athletic Association. His sister was the novelist Myrtle Beatrice Strode-Jackson.

Educated at Malvern College, Jackson entered Brasenose College, Oxford in 1910, where he took a degree in law and rowed and played football and hockey for the College. He won the mile race for Oxford against Cambridge three times and was President of the Oxford University Athletic Club.

In 1912, while still an undergraduate, Jackson cut short his fishing holiday in Norway, and travelled by train to compete in that year's Olympic Games in Stockholm. Having not been chosen by the Great Britain team, he had to compete as a private entry. Stockholm was the last Olympics at which such private entries were allowed.

Even when compared to the amateurish race preparation of the era, Jackson's training regime of massage, golf and walking seemed very relaxed. American hopes were high to win a gold in the 1500 metres, as the USA dominated middle-distance running at that time, and seven of the runners in the final were from the USA.

In what was described at the time as, 'The greatest race ever run', in a dramatic finish, Jackson managed to beat both the world record-holder for the 1500 metres and the mile record-holder.

Aged just twenty-one, Jackson thus became the youngest-ever Olympic 1500m gold medallist until Kenyan Asbel Kiprop in 2008, who was 19.

At the outbreak of the Great War, Jackson was commissioned in the Royal North Lancashire Regiment and, in September 1914, was attached to the 13th (Service) Battalion, The Rifle Brigade, as a second lieutenant. He went over to France with the battalion and was with them until promoted lieutenant colonel in May 1918, when he took command of the 13th Battalion, The King's Royal Rifle Corps.

In December 1914, he was promoted to temporary lieutenant and in July 1916, he was promoted to captain. He was made an acting major in June 1917 and in August, acting lieutenant colonel. He was made a full lieutenant colonel in May 1918, and acting brigadier in October 1918. He was wounded three times and left permanently lame, so the war put an end to his sporting career. His DSO citations read as follows:

DSO, June 1917: only a general citation given.

For his 1st Bar, July 1917:

> "for conspicuous gallantry during lengthy operations, when he assumed command of the battalion and, although wounded on two separate occasions, was able to carry out most valuable work. By his skill and courage he offered a splendid example to all ranks with him."

2nd Bar, May 1918:

> "for conspicuous gallantry and devotion to duty. His

battalion was subjected to an intense bombardment throughout a whole day, which caused many casualties and cut off all communication by wire with the front-line companies. He handles the situation with such skill and initiative that when the enemy attacked towards evening the casualties caused by the bombardment had been evacuated and replaced by reinforcements and communication with the front line had been re-established. It was entirely due to his powers of command and the splendid spirit with which he inspired his men that the attack on the greater part of his front was repulsed, and that the enemy, though they penetrated into parts of the front line, were counter-attacked and held at bay until the arrival of reinforcements. By his skilful dispositions he materially assisted the counter-attack which finally drove the enemy back with heavy losses and completely re-established the position."

3rd Bar, December 1918:

"for conspicuous gallantry and brilliant leadership. During an attack by our troops Lt-Col Jackson advanced with the leading wave of his battalion and was among the first to reach the railway embankment. The machine-gun fire against them was intense, but the gallant leading of this officer gave such impetus to the assault that the enemy's main line of resistance was broken. He was subsequently wounded during the work of consolidation."

Jackson was also Mentioned in Despatches six times during the war.

He was a member of the British delegation at the Paris Peace

Conference, 1919 and was awarded the CBE, before he was called to the Bar at Middle Temple. He went on to be a member of the British Olympic Council in 1920, and a major force in the founding of the Achilles Club, a renowned athletics club for former Oxford and Cambridge athletes.

Jackson emigrated to the United States in 1921, where he worked in industry and as a Justice of the Peace in Connecticut. He directed the first Kentucky Derby Festival in 1935. During World War Two, he was a colonel on the staff of the Governor of Kentucky. He became a U.S. citizen in 1945, but later returned to Oxford where he died in 1972 aged 81.

Robert Sinclair Knox DSO
The Derry Volunteers of the 36th (Ulster) Division

Robert Sinclair Knox was born near Coleraine, County Antrim in 1881. When the First World War broke out, he volunteered to serve in the 10th Battalion of the Royal Inniskilling Fusiliers (the Derry Volunteers), part of the 109th (Inniskilling) Brigade of the 36th (Ulster) Division. He arrived in France in October 1915 and was promoted to major in June 1916.

Knox's DSO was gazetted in January 1917. He was also wounded and Mentioned in Despatches. He saw action at the Third Battle of Ypres (Passchendaele) and the Battle of Cambrai. He was awarded his first Bar to his DSO in February 1918.

He commanded the 10th (Service) Battalion of the Royal Inniskilling Fusiliers in 1917, and then the 9th Battalion in 1918. He fought in the German Spring Offensive near St Quentin in March 1918, where his battalion suffered heavy casualties. He received a second Bar to his DSO, gazetted in September 1918.

Knox won a third Bar to his DSO in March 1919. Two other officers were awarded a third Bar at the same time, Archibald Walter Buckle and William 'Bob' Dawson. An award of the Croix de Guerre was gazetted in June 1919.

Knox became Deputy Lieutenant for County Londonderry in August 1938 and served as a lieutenant colonel in the Royal Engineers in the Second World War, before retiring in 1949. He died in 1963 at the age of 81.

Edward Allan Wood CMG DSO
6th Battalion of the King's Shropshire Light Infantry

Edward Allan Wood was born in India, the ninth son of Oswald Wood, a civil servant who later became a judge. Family resources were limited, and Wood joined the British Army as a private soldier in 1892, first enlisting in the 2nd Dragoon Guards and later transferring to the 17th Lancers. He served as an officer in the Bechuanaland Border Police (Botswana Police Service), the Matabeleland Mounted Police and the British South Africa Police, in the 1890s. He joined the Bechuanaland Border Police column in the Jameson Raid against the South African Republic in 1895 and was captured in the Transvaal. He served with the Matabeleland Relief Force during the rebellion in 1896. He later served in the Second Boer War in 1899–1902 and was present at the relief of Mafeking in 1900. He resigned from the British South Africa Police in March 1906.

At the outbreak of the First World War in 1914, Wood rejoined the British Army and became a company commander in 6th Battalion of the King's Shropshire Light Infantry. He became a temporary lieutenant colonel in 1917 and won the DSO and a Bar while commanding the 6th Battalion. Wood was promoted to brigadier general to command the 55th Infantry Brigade in the 18th (Eastern) Division in November 1917. A second Bar was announced in September 1918, and third Bar in December 1919.

He was appointed a Companion of the Order of St Michael and St George (CMG) in the January 1919 New Year's Honours List and also received the Croix de Guerre.

Wood was demobilised in early 1919, and he joined the Auxiliary

Division of the Royal Irish Constabulary in October 1919 and took command in February 1921. He died in London in May 1930 at the age of 65 and is buried in Highgate Cemetery.

Also from the King's Shropshire Light Infantry, Captain Ernest Robert Maling English (1874-1941) was educated at Wellington College and the Royal Military College, Sandhurst. He played cricket for Gloucestershire and played once for England in 1909. Captain English received his commission in 1895 and served in the Second Anglo-Boer War (during which he was wounded). He was promoted to captain in 1909 and major in 1915. During his First World War service, he was wounded again and was awarded the DSO (in 1917), the Croix de Guerre and twice Mentioned in Despatches. He retired from the Army with the rank of lieutenant colonel on 29 November 1919. After leaving the Army, Ernest English became an actor, performing on stage and screen.

Oswald Cuthbert Borrett, son of Major General Herbert Borrett was born in March 1878 and joined the King's Own Royal Lancaster Regiment on 7th May 1898. He served in the South African War (1899-1902) and was promoted Major on 22nd October 1914 and he served with the 2nd Battalion King's Own in France from January 1915. He was award the DSO for an action on 18th February, 1915:

"While the fighting in front of the German barricade was at its height, Major Borrett came face to face with the German officer. Raising their revolvers they fired point blank at each other. In a moment the German fell dead, while Major Borrett, who was hit in the shoulder, dropped his weapon."

Borrett was later wounded in August 1915, but returned to service and commanded the 1st Battalion King's Own and later took command of three Infantry Brigades in France.

The Victoria Cross (VC)

The Victoria Cross is the most prestigious and evocative of all the British gallantry awards. It is given for, "...most conspicuous bravery, or some daring or pre-eminent act of valour or self-sacrifice, or extreme devotion to duty in the presence of the enemy."

In 1854, in the midst of the Crimean War, at the opening of Parliament Queen Victoria paid tribute to the soldiers of her 'unconquerable Army' and expressed her admiration and gratitude to them. Later that year, Capt. G.T. Scobell, M.P. made a formal proposal to the House of Commons, "...that an humble address be presented to Her Majesty ... to institute an Order of Merit to be bestowed upon persons serving in the Army or Navy for distinguished and prominent personal gallantry during the present war and to which every grade and individual... may be

Bhanbhagta Gurung, a Rifleman with the 3rd Battalion of the 2nd Gurkha Rifles holds the Victoria Cross he was awarded with whilst fighting in Burma during the Second World War.

Queen Victoria in 1855 reviewing veterans of the Crimean War, 1855.

admissible."

As described in the introduction above, at that time officers involved in conflict could be recognised via the Order of the Bath, an award founded by George I in 1725, but no such award was available to acknowledge the heroic actions of the ordinary British serviceman. An assurance was given by the Government that a new order was indeed under consideration and, as a result of further questioning on the matter, the Prime Minister gave an answer to the House of Commons on March 19th 1855 declaring that Her Majesty's Government fully intended to establish such an order.

The introduction of a medal had the full support of both Queen Victoria and Prince Albert and they were both closely involved with its development. The original Royal Warrant for the Victoria Cross stated clearly that this new award was being, "...ordained with a view to place all persons on a perfectly equal footing in relation to eligibility for the Decoration, that neither rank, nor long service, nor wounds, nor any other circumstance or condition whatsoever, save the merit of conspicuous bravery shall be held to establish a sufficient claim to the honour."

Various designs were presented to the Queen, which she would return with her comments and amendments. Finally, on January 5th 1856 a design was approved with one final alteration. Her Majesty preferred that the motto on the Cross stated, 'For Valour' rather than 'For the Brave' as this would lead to the inference that only those who have been awarded the Cross are deemed 'brave.'

Having approved the design on paper, the first metal proof was submitted to the Queen on February 4th but was rejected. A revised proof was submitted on the February 21st with more amendments being made. Further proofs were subsequently created until, on March 3rd 1856, the matter was finalised when the samples were returned, with one having been chosen as satisfactory.

The bronze from which all Victoria Crosses are made was thought to have come from cannons captured from the Russians at Sebastopol during the Crimean War. However, it seems the cannons may not have been Russian. 1990s research by historian John Glanfield and analysis by metallurgists, Dudley Creagh and John Ashton, has established that the metal for the medals came from two Chinese cannon and that there is no evidence of Russian origin. A likely explanation is that the cannon were taken as British trophies during the First Opium War against the Qing Dynasty (1839 –1842).

The cannon are on display at The Royal Artillery Museum at Woolwich. The remaining portion (about 10kgs) of the only remaining cascabel (muzzle-loading cannon), is stored in a vault maintained by 15 Regiment Royal Logistic Corps at Donnington. It can only be removed under armed guard. It is estimated that approximately 80 to 85 more VCs could be cast from this source.

VCs have been made by Hancocks of London since they were first introduced. Unlike any other award for gallantry, the VC is not made by a die. It is not struck, as are coins and many other medals, it is cast. The cannon's gunmetal proved to be so hard that the dies which were used began to crack, so it was decided to cast the medals instead, a chance circumstance which resulted in a higher relief and more depth in the moulding than would have been possible with a die-stamped medal.

The medal is sand-cast in moulds usually containing four specimens at a time. The suspension bar is cast at the same time. The obverse, reverse and suspension bar are hand chased to the minutest detail and the whole medal has a special bronze finish applied at the end of the process to darken the colour. Twelve Victoria Crosses are produced at a time.

Paradoxically, this most glamorous of awards is probably the least ostentatious in design. The medal is a cross pattée ('footed cross', where the arms of the cross are broader at the end than in the centre) in bronze, which does not glint like most medals, but has a patina of respectful antiquity.

The obverse has the royal crest of a lion astride a crown above a scroll inscribed, 'FOR VALOUR'. The reverse is plain except for a central roundel, which bears the date of the action for which the award is made.

The medal's suspension bar is a laurelled bronze bar ending in a 'V', from which a plain ring is attached to the medal. The reverse of the suspension bar bears a light engraving of the recipient's name and details. The ribbon was originally dark red, sometimes referred to as crimson or 'wine-red' for the Army, dark blue for the Navy and Marines, but, from 1918, became dark red for all services. Bars for further acts of valour were authorised by the original royal warrant, but, to date, only three Bars have ever been awarded.

The VC is also a very rare distinction, with only 1,358 awarded since its inception in 1856. Because of its rarity, the medal has fetched over £400,000 at auction and a number of public and private collections are devoted to it. The private collection of Lord Ashcroft, amassed since 1986, contains 162 medals, almost 12% of all VCs awarded. Following a 2008 £5 million donation to the Imperial War Museum, his collection went on public display alongside the museum's Victoria and George Cross collection in November 2010.

On June 21st 1854, onboard HMS Hecla, Mate Charles Davis Lucas performed the act which was later to earn him the honour of becoming the first winner of the Victoria Cross. While attacking the Russian fortress at Bomarsund in the Aland Islands, a live shell landed on the deck of the Hecla. Disregarding orders to take

Colonel John Rouse Merriott Chard VC (21 December 1847 – 1 November 1897) received his Victoria Cross for his role in the defence of Rorke's Drift in January 1879 where he commanded a small British garrison of 139 soldiers that successfully repulsed an assault by some 3,000 to 4,000 Zulu warriors. The battle was recreated in the film Zulu in which Chard was portrayed by Stanley Baker. At the end of the war he returned to a hero's welcome in England and was invited to an audience with Queen Victoria.

cover, Lucas picked up the shell with its fuse still burning and calmly walked to the edge of the ship before dropping it over the side, the shell exploded as it hit the water. Thus, the standard of heroism was set for others to follow.

In its early years, awards of the new honour were prolific, with more VCs awarded to soldiers who fought to suppress the Indian Mutiny than to the soldiers who fought in the Second World War. In just one day alone, on November 16th 1857 at the Relief of Lucknow, no less than 24 VCs were awarded.

In 1879, at Rorke's Drift, Natal, during the Anglo-Zulu War, a small British contingent of only 137 men stood firm against a vast army of Zulu warriors. For that one single battle, eleven VCs were awarded.

The youngest recipients recorded are: Hospital Apprentice A. Fitzgibbon, Indian Medical Establishment, who was 15 years and 3

Private Johnson Beharry, one of the most recent recipients of the Victoria Cross, was awarded his on 18 March 2005, for saving members of his unit, the 1st Battalion Princess of Wales's Royal Regiment, from ambushes on 1 May and again on 11 June 2004 at Al-Amarah, Iraq. He sustained serious head injuries in the latter engagement. Beharry was formally invested with the Victoria Cross by Queen Elizabeth II on 27 April 2005.

months, at the Battle of Taku Forts, China, in 1861 and Boy 1st Class J. T. Cornwell, RN who was 16 years 4 months at the Battle of Jutland in 1916, (posthumous). The oldest recipient was Captain W. Raynor, Bengal Veteran Establishment, Siege of Delhi, Indian Mutiny, 1857. Raynor was 61.

633 VCs were awarded during the Great War and 182 during the Second World War. Only thirteen VCs have been awarded since the end of the Second World War.

One of the most recent being presented to Grenada-born soldier Johnson Beharry of the Princess of Wales's Royal Regiment, for actions in Iraq. In 2004, when exposed to ferocious enemy fire, Private Beharry steered his own Warrior armoured vehicle away from an ambush, leading five other Warriors to safety. Beharry suffered a head injury as a result. Returning to duty the following month, he again suffered a serious head injury whilst reversing his Warrior out of yet another ambush. In addition to saving his own life, Private Beharry undoubtedly saved the lives of his injured commander and the other crew members of the Warrior.

Whilst still recovering from brain surgery, Private Beharry was presented with his award by the Queen in April 2005, who apparently told him, "It's been rather a long time since I've awarded one of these."

The most recent award was to Joshua Mark Leakey, a British soldier currently serving in the Parachute Regiment. The actions for which Leakey was awarded the VC occurred on August 22nd 2013 in Helmand Province, Afghanistan. The Ministry of Defence summarised his citation as follows: "Under fire yet undeterred by the very clear and present danger, Lance Corporal Leakey ran across the exposed slope of the hill three times to initiate casualty evacuation, re-site machine guns and return fire. His actions proved the turning point, inspiring his comrades to fight back with renewed ferocity. Displaying gritty leadership well above that expected of his rank, Lance Corporal Leakey's actions singlehandedly regained the initiative and prevented considerable loss of life."

The VC has never been awarded to a woman. However, a gold representation of the decoration, without the wording on the scroll, was presented to Elizabeth Webber Harris, the wife of the commanding officer, 104th Bengal Fusiliers, by the officers of the Regiment for her actions during a cholera outbreak.

In October 1868, the newly-promoted Major General Webber Harris took his men to Peshawar, having anticipated trouble on India's north-west frontier. However, in 1869 cholera swept India and by August the soldiers were infected. In September, part of the regiment went to a temporary camp in the countryside, with the remaining soldiers joining them five days later. By then, many soldiers and their families had already died from the disease and Mrs Harris was the only woman to go with them.

In her mid-30s at the time, she spent three months nursing the sick and keeping up their spirits, moving through the baking Indian countryside to take care of the regiment as they moved stations. One night she was attacked by two tribesmen who seized her horse in an incident she described as 'alarming'.

The officers of the Regiment felt Mrs Harris had lived up to the traditions of the Victoria Cross and in 1869 she was awarded with the honorary medal. A letter to the Times stated: "It is said that it was suggested to Queen Victoria that Mrs Webber Harris might be given the Victoria Cross, but this was, of course, not possible, so the gold replica was made and presented to her instead." Mrs Harris later wrote: "It is a most beautiful ornament, and will always be my most cherished possession."

She died in London in 1917 at the age of 83. In 2015, her medal was acquired by Lord Ashcroft and became part of the Imperial War Museum VC collection.

Only three people have been awarded the VC and Bar. They are: Noel Chavasse and Arthur Martin-Leake, both doctors in the Royal Army Medical Corps for rescuing wounded under fire; and New Zealander Charles Upham, an infantryman, for valour in combat.

Noel Godfrey Chavasse VC
Royal Army Medical Corps

Noel Godfrey Chavasse was born in Oxford in November, 1884. His father, Francis Chavasse, became Bishop of Liverpool in 1900. He was educated at Liverpool College and Trinity College, Oxford. After graduating with first class honours in 1907 he studied medicine. In 1908, Chavasse and his twin brother, Christopher, both represented Britain in the London Olympic Games in the 400 metres. Noel finished third in his heat, while Christopher finished second, but only the heat winners progressed to the semi-finals.

Chavasse worked in Dublin and the Royal Southern Hospital

in Liverpool before joining the Royal Army Medical Corps in 1913. At the outbreak of the Great War, Chavasse volunteered to serve in France. He was transferred to the Western Front in November 1914, where he was attached to the Liverpool Scottish Regiment. In the first few months Chavasse was kept busy dealing with trench foot, a condition caused by standing for long periods in mud and water.

In March 1915 the regiment took part in the offensive at Ypres, where poison gas was used for the first time. By June 1915 only 142 men out of the 829 men who arrived with Chavasse remained on active duty. The rest had been killed or badly wounded.

Chavasse was promoted to captain in August 1915 and six months later was awarded the Military Cross for his actions at the Battle of Hooge. In April 1916 he was granted three days leave to receive his award from King George V.

In July 1916, Chavasse's battalion was moved to the Somme battlefield near Mametz. On August 7th, the Liverpool Scottish were ordered to attack Guillemont. Of the 620 men who took part in the offensive, 106 of the men were killed and 174 were wounded. This included Chavasse who was hit by shell splinters while rescuing men in no-mans-land. For this he was awarded the VC. The citation reads:

> For most conspicuous bravery and devotion to duty.
>
> "During an attack he tended the wounded in the open all day, under heavy fire, frequently in view of the enemy. During the ensuing night he searched for wounded on

the ground in front of the enemy's lines for four hours.

Next day he took one stretcher-bearer to the advanced trenches, and under heavy shell fire carried an urgent case for 500 yards into safety, being wounded in the side by a shell splinter during the journey. The same night he took up a party of twenty volunteers, rescued three wounded men from a shell hole twenty-five yards from the enemy's trench, buried the bodies of two officers, and collected many identity discs, although fired on by bombs and machine guns.

Altogether he saved the lives of some twenty badly wounded men, besides the ordinary cases which passed through his hands. His courage and self-sacrifice, were beyond praise."

Chavasse's second award was made during the period 31 July to 2 August 1917, at Wieltje, Belgium and reads:

His Majesty the King has been graciously pleased to approve of the award of a Bar to the Victoria Cross to Capt. Noel Godfrey Chavasse, V.C., M.C., late, R.A.M.C.

"For most conspicuous bravery and devotion to duty when in action.

Though severely wounded early in the action whilst carrying a wounded soldier to the Dressing Station, Capt. Chavasse refused to leave his post, and for two days not only continued to perform his duties, but in addition went out repeatedly under heavy fire to search for and attend to the wounded who were lying out. During these searches, although practically without food during this period, worn with fatigue and faint with his wound, he assisted to carry in a number of badly wounded men, over heavy and difficult ground. By his extraordinary energy and inspiring example, he was instrumental in rescuing many wounded who would have otherwise undoubtedly succumbed under the bad weather conditions."

After being badly wounded, Chavasse was sent to the Casualty Clearing Station at Brandhoek. Although operated on, he died on August 4th 1917.

Captain Chavasse's service and gallantry medals were donated by his family decades ago to St Peter's College, Oxford. In November 2009 it was announced that the college had sold the medals to Lord Ashcroft, the Tory peer who has a collection of over 160 Victoria Crosses. According to college sources, the price was "close to £1.5 million", easily topping the previous world record for a medal, rumoured to be a private sale worth £1 million.

Lord Aschcroft has also donated £5 million to the Imperial War Museum to create a Gallery in which his collection of VCs and other medals owned by the museum can be put on display to the public.

Arthur Martin-Leake VC
5th Field Ambulance, Royal Army Medical Corps

Arthur, the fifth son of Stephen Martin-Leake of Thorpe Hall, Essex was educated at Westminster School before studying medicine at University College Hospital, qualifying in 1893. He was employed at Hemel Hempstead District Hospital before enlisting in the Imperial Yeomanry, to serve in the Boer War in 1899.

He was 27 years old and a surgeon captain in the South African Constabulary attached to the 5th Field Ambulance during the Second Boer War in February 1902, at Vlakfontein when he was awarded his first VC. The citation reads:

> "During the action at Vlakfontein, on the 8th February, 1902, Surgeon-Captain Martin-Leake went up to a wounded man, and attended to him under heavy fire from about 40 Boers at 100 yards range. He then went to the assistance of a wounded officer, and, whilst trying to place him in a comfortable position, was shot three times, but would not give in till he rolled over thoroughly exhausted. All the eight men at this point were wounded, and while they were lying on the Veldt, Surgeon-Captain Martin-Leake refused water till everyone else had been served."

Martin-Leake qualified as a Fellow of the Royal College of Surgeons in 1903 after studying while convalescing from his wounds. He then took up an appointment in India as Chief Medical Officer with the Bengal-Nagpur Railway.

In 1912, he volunteered to serve with the British Red Cross during the Balkan Wars, attached to the Montenegrin army, and was

present during the Siege of Scutari (1912–13) and at Tarabosh Mountain. He was awarded the Order of the Montenegrin Red Cross.

At the outbreak of the Great War, Martin-Leake returned to service as a lieutenant with the 5th Field Ambulance, Royal Army Medical Corps, on the Western Front.

He was awarded his second VC, aged 40, during the period

October 29th to November 8th 1914 near Zonnebeke, Belgium. His award citation reads:

> "Lieutenant Arthur Martin Leake, Royal Army Medical Corps, who was awarded the Victoria Cross on 13th May, 1902, is granted a Clasp for conspicuous bravery in the present campaign for most conspicuous bravery and devotion to duty throughout the campaign, especially during the period 29th October to 8th November, 1914, near Zonnebeke, in rescuing, whilst exposed to constant fire, a large number of the wounded who were lying close to the enemy's trenches."

He was promoted to captain in March 1915, major in November the same year, and in April 1917 took command of 46th Field Ambulance with the rank of lieutenant colonel. Martin-Leake retired from the army after the war and resumed his company employment in India until he retired to England in 1937. During the Second World War, he commanded an ARP (Air Raid Precautions) post. He died in 1953 aged 79, at High Cross, Hertfordshire.

Charles Hazlitt Upham VC

20th Canterbury-Otago Battalion, 2nd New Zealand Expeditionary Force

Charles Hazlitt Upham became New Zealand's most famous soldier for his actions during the Second World War, when he was awarded the VC and Bar, becoming the only person to have achieved this as a combat soldier.

Born in Christchurch in 1908, Upham joined the 2nd New Zealand Expeditionary Force soon after war broke out in September 1939.

Upham earned his VC for outstanding gallantry and leadership in Crete in May 1941, the citation reporting:

> During the operations in Crete this officer performed a series of remarkable exploits, showing outstanding leadership, tactical skill and utter indifference to danger.

> He commanded a forward platoon in the attack on Maleme on 22nd May and fought his way forward for over 3,000 yards unsupported by any other arms and against a defence strongly organised in depth. During this operation his platoon destroyed numerous enemy posts but on three occasions sections were temporarily held up.

> In the first case, under a heavy fire from a machine gun nest he advanced to close quarters with pistol and grenades, so demoralizing the occupants that his section was able to "mop up" with ease.

> Another of his sections was then held up by two machine

guns in a house. He went in and placed a grenade through a window, destroying the crew of one machine gun and several others, the other machine gun being silenced by the fire of his sections.

In the third case he crawled to within 15 yards of an M.G. post and killed the gunners with a grenade.

When his Company withdrew from Maleme he helped to carry a wounded man out under fire, and together with another officer rallied more men together to carry other wounded men out.

He was then sent to bring in a company which had become isolated. With a Corporal he went through enemy territory over 600 yards, killing two Germans on the way, found the company, and brought it back to the Battalion's new position. But for this action it would have been completely cut off.

During the following two days his platoon occupied an exposed position on forward slopes and was continuously under fire. Second Lieutenant Upham was blown over by one mortar shell, and painfully wounded by a piece of shrapnel behind the left shoulder, by another. He disregarded this wound and remained on duty. He also received a bullet in the foot which he later removed in Egypt.

At Galatas on 25th May his platoon was heavily engaged and came under severe mortar and machine-gun fire. While his platoon stopped under cover of a ridge Second-

Lieutenant Upham went forward, observed the enemy and brought the platoon forward when the Germans advanced. They killed over 40 with fire and grenades and forced the remainder to fall back.

When his platoon was ordered to retire he sent it back under the platoon Sergeant and he went back to warn other troops that they were being cut off. When he came out himself he was fired on by two Germans. He fell and shammed dead, then crawled into a position and having the use of only one arm rested his rifle in the fork of a tree and as the Germans came forward he killed them both. The second to fall actually hit the muzzle of the

A VC award ceremony in the desert at Baggush 35 miles east of Mersa Matruh in the Western Desert, 4 November 1941: from left, Lt Charles Upham, Lt Col Howard Kippenberger, Major Raymond Lynch. It was Kippenberger who lobbied for Upham to receive the second award of the VC, telling King George VI "In my respectful opinion, Sir, Upham won the VC several times over."

rifle as he fell.

On 30th May at Sphakia his platoon was ordered to deal with a party of the enemy which had advanced down a ravine to near Force Headquarters. Though in an exhausted condition he climbed the steep hill to the west of the ravine, placed his men in positions on the slope overlooking the ravine and himself went to the top with a Bren Gun and two riflemen. By clever tactics he induced the enemy party to expose itself and then at a range of 500 yards shot 22 and caused the remainder to disperse in panic.

During the whole of the operations he suffered from dysentery and was able to eat very little, in addition to being wounded and bruised.

He showed superb coolness, great skill and dash and complete disregard of danger. His conduct and leadership inspired his whole platoon to fight magnificently throughout, and in fact was an inspiration to the Battalion.

He earned his second VC (awarded as a Bar) at Ruweisat Ridge, Egypt, in July 1942, although the award of the Bar took three years to be agreed. After being severely wounded in the latter engagement, Upham was captured by the Germans. After a failed escape attempt while recuperating in an Italian hospital, he was transferred to Germany in September 1943. A particularly audacious solo attempt to scale his camp's barbed-wire fences in broad daylight saw Upham become the only New Zealand combatant officer sent to the infamous Colditz camp for habitual escapers in 1944. He remained a prisoner there until he was liberated by the Allied advance in 1945.

After Upham's capture, his fellow officers began collecting evidence to support the award of a bar to his Victoria Cross. But the British hierarchy thought Upham should be made a DSO. It was decided to leave the matter until his release. In July 1945, General Bernard Freyberg Commander of the NZEF, revived the question and further evidence was gathered by Major-General Howard Kippenberger and it was decided that his actions merited the highest recognition possible.

When the recommendation for his second VC was made later in 1945 King George VI said to Kippenberger that a Bar to the cross would be "very unusual indeed." The King inquired, "Does he deserve it?", to which Kippenberger replied, "In my respectful opinion, Sir, Upham won the VC several times over."

After the war, Upham returned to farming life in Canterbury, where he died in 1994 at the age of 86.